Letter to Caregivers

T0017018

Dear Caregivers,

This workbook is organized into seven stages that each focus on a set of letters. For example, Stage 1 includes the letters **s, a, t, i,** and **m**. In each stage, the child will learn letter sounds, practice writing upper and lower case letters, build spelling skills, read "heart" words, and play games to reinforce phonics skills.

When the child learns a new letter sound, be sure to model the correct way to make the sound. Have the child watch your mouth as you make the sound, then have them practice. It is helpful to have them look at their mouth in a mirror as they make the sound so they can see the placement of their mouth, lips, and tongue. When modeling consonant sounds, ensure the child clips the sounds and does not add a /uh/ sound after them. For example, the /b/ sound should only be /b/, not /buh/, and their mouth should only open slightly.

As you work with the child, it is important to emphasize the letter-sound relationship consistently. This helps them match the written letter (visual) with the sound the letter represents (auditory). Some activities start with written letter(s) and ask the child to say the sounds. This is called decoding, or reading. Other activities ask the child to say the word or sounds first and then write or spell the letters. This is called encoding, or spelling.

As the child learns new letter sounds, be sure to have them collect the corresponding stickers and add them to the journey map on **pages 6–7**.

In each stage, the child will practice reading and spelling "heart" words. Heart words have regular and irregular parts. The child can sound out the regular parts because they make the sound the child has learned. For example, the **i** in the word "is" makes the short /i/ sound. The child will need help reading the irregular parts because they do not follow the sound they have learned. In the same example, the **s** in "is" makes the /z/ sound. As the child reads and spells heart words, ensure that they know the irregular parts and that they "learn them by heart."

the

- Sound buttons are used to help identify individual sounds in words. Dots are used to show separate sounds. Lines are used under two or more letters that represent one sound.

- Hearts are used to identify the tricky part of the word that must be "learned by heart."

Lastly, look for the "Tips" throughout the workbook for suggestions on how to reinforce the letter-sound relationship, to model forming the mouth when making sounds, or to practice phonics skills through word games.

Happy Reading!

Contents

4

Letter Sounds Journey Map

Fill this page with stickers as you complete the stages.

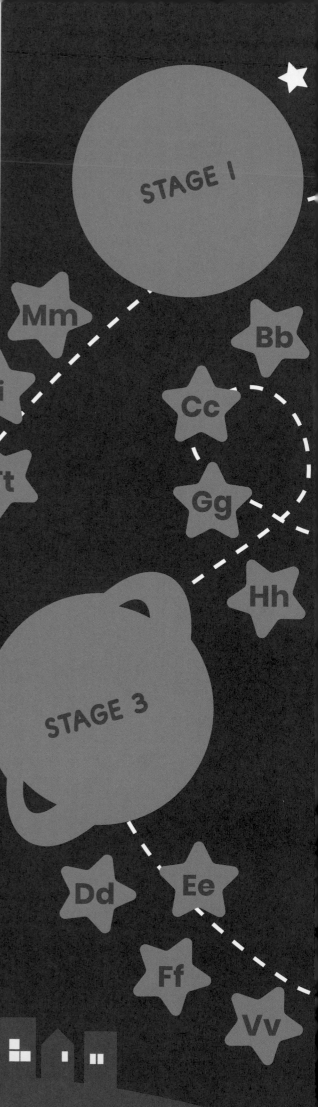

STAGE 1

Mm

Bb

Ii

Cc

Aa

Tt

Gg

Ss

Hh

STAGE 3

Dd

Ee

Ff

Vv

Ss

Say the letter sound.

Check ✔ all the things that start with the /s/ sound.

Trace the upper case S.

Copy the upper case S.

Trace the lower case s.

Copy the lower case s.

TIP

Encourage the child to say the sound as they write each letter. Saying the sound and forming the letter at the same time solidifies the letter–sound correspondence skill.

Aa

Say the letter sound.

Color all the things that start with the /a/ sound.

Letter formation a

Trace the upper case A.

A A A A A

Copy the upper case A.

A

Trace the lower case a.

a a a a

Copy the lower case a.

a

The /t/ sound

Tt

Say the letter sound.

Circle all the things that start with the /t/ sound.

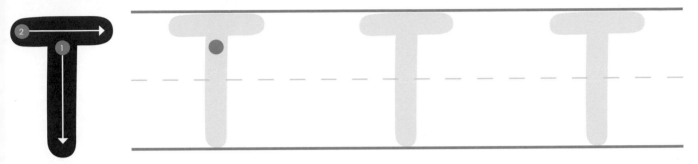

Letter formation **t**

Trace the upper case T.

Copy the upper case T.

Trace the lower case t.

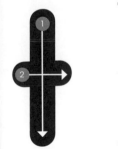

Copy the lower case t.

Ii

Say the letter sound.

Circle all the things that start with the /i/ sound.

Trace the upper case I.

Copy the upper case I.

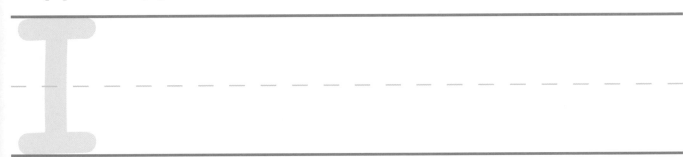

Trace the lower case i.

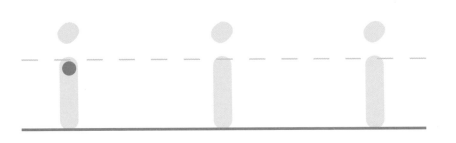

Copy the lower case i.

Mm

Say the letter sound.

Help Lin the monkey get to the bananas by following all the things that start with the /m/ sound.

Trace the upper case M.

Copy the upper case M.

Trace the lower case m.

Copy the lower case m.

Here are 10 things that start with a /s/, /a/, /t/, /i/, or /m/ sound. Which of these things can you find in the big picture?

Check ✓ the things you find.

Color each shape with a thing that starts with a /s/, /a/, /t/, /i/, or /m/ sound.

Match the upper case letter to the lower case letter.

 S

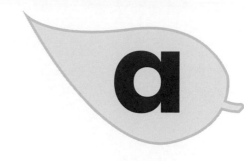 a

 A

 i

T

 m

I

 s

 M

 t

Match the lower case letter to the upper case letter.

Fill in the missing sound.

 __ a t

 __ i t

 __ a t

Fill in the missing sound.

 s __ t

 s __ t

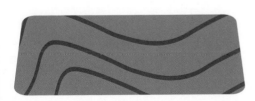 m __ t

Fill in the missing sound.

s a __

m a __

s i __

Fill in all the missing sounds.

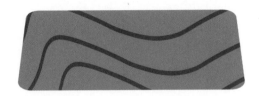

_____   _____   _____

_____   _____   _____

_____   _____   _____

Trace the words to help the animals get to the food.

the

a

of

TIP

Heart words contain irregular and regular spelling patterns. The irregular part of a word has a heart under it because the child must learn the sound "by heart."

Trace the word. Then read the word.

the   the   the

Copy the word.

Trace the word. Then read the word.

a   a   a

Copy the word.

Trace the word. Then read the word.

of   of   of

Copy the word.

Trace the word. Then read the word.

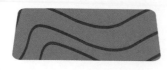

mat   mat

Copy the word.

Trace the word. Then read the word.

sit   sit

Copy the word.

Trace the word. Then read the word.

sat   sat

Copy the word.

Trace the words to make sentences. Then read the sentences.

It is Tim.

Sit, Tim.

Tim sat on the mat.

Snake game

For 1 to 4 players. You will need tokens and a die. Take turns rolling the die and moving your token. Read the word you land on. If you land on a snake tail, move up the snake to its head. If you land on a snake head, move down the snake to its tail.

TIP

If the child is not able to read the word, help them sound it out. Example: you say /s/ /a/ /t/ and have them put together the sounds to read the word.

Start	Tam	Sat		Sam
Sam		it	the	sit
Tam	on	it		Tim
mat	Sam	on	is	Tam
sat	is		the	Finish

Congratulations!

Now you know your **s a t i m** sounds.

Well done!

Collect a planet sticker to add to your journey map.

STAGE 1
COMPLETE

Have you collected all of your letter sound stars from the sticker page?

Ss Aa Tt Ii Mm

Nn

Say the letter sound.

Check ✓ **all the things that start with the /n/ sound.**

Trace the upper case N.

Copy the upper case N.

N

Trace the lower case n.

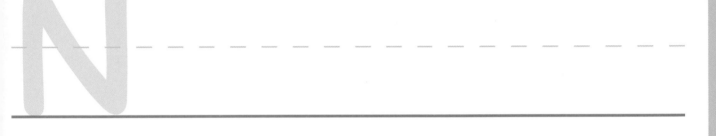

Copy the lower case n.

n

Say the letter sound.

Circle the thing in each row that starts with the /o/ sound.

Trace the upper case O.

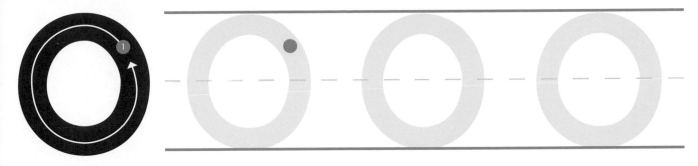

Copy the upper case O.

Trace the lower case o.

Copy the lower case o.

P p

Say the letter sound.

Color all the things that start with the /p/ sound.

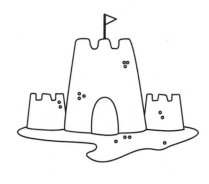

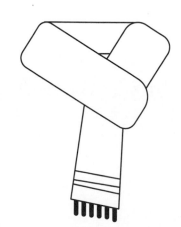

Trace the upper case P.

Copy the upper case P.

Trace the lower case p.

Copy the lower case p.

Sorting sounds

Here are 10 things that start with a /n/, /o/, or /p/ sound. Which of these things can you find in the big picture?

Check the things you find.

Color each section that has a thing that starts with a /n/, /o/, or /p/ sound.

Match the upper case letter to the lower case letter.

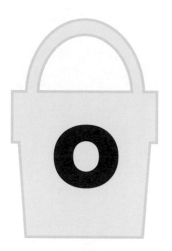

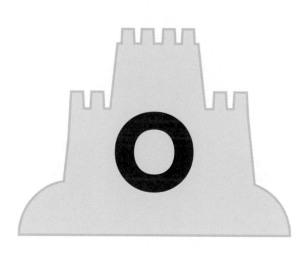

Match the lower case letter to the upper case letter.

Fill in the missing sound.

___ a p

___ o t

___ o p

Fill in the missing sound.

TIP

Have the child say what's in the picture. Ask "What sound do you hear at the beginning?" Then ask "What makes that sound?" Have them write the letter and read the word.

 __ o p

 __ a p

 __ a n

43

Fill in the missing sound.

p _ p

n _ p

m _ p

Fill in the missing sound.

t __ p

p __ t

p __ n

Fill in the missing sound.

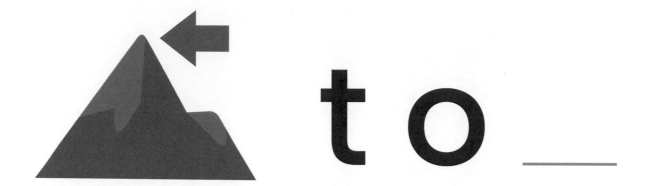

t o __

m a __

p o __

Fill in the missing sound.

 p o __

 p a __

 n a __

STAGE 2 : n o p

Fill in all the missing sounds.

_____ _____ _____

_____ _____ _____

_____ _____ _____

48

Fill in all the missing sounds.

_____ _____ _____

_____ _____ _____

_____ _____ _____

Trace the words to help the pirates get to the treasure.

Trace the word. Then read the word.

all   all   all

Copy the word.

Trace the word. Then read the word.

from from

Copy the word.

Trace the word. Then read the word.

one   one   one

Copy the word.

Trace the word. Then read the word.

nap nap

Copy the word.

Trace the word. Then read the word.

pop pop

Copy the word.

Trace the word. Then read the word.

top top

Copy the word.

Writing sentences

Trace the words to make sentences. Then read the sentences.

It is Pam.

Pam has one mat.

Pam has a nap.

Sticker game

Find the stickers of things that start with a /n/, /o/, or /p/ sound. Match the stickers with the correct words on the picture below.

TIP

Play word games for extra practice. Ask, "Which word doesn't belong?" Then give two words that start with the same sound and one that starts with a different sound (example: "nap," "chair," "note").

Pam

necklace

octopus

Congratulations!

Now you know your
n o p sounds.

Well done!

Collect a planet
sticker to add to
your journey map.

STAGE 2 COMPLETE

Have you collected all of
your letter sound stars
from the sticker page?

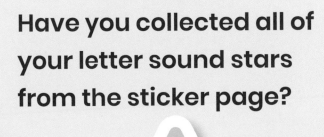

Nn   Oo   Pp

The /b/ sound

Bb

Say the letter sound.

Get Bell the bee to the honey by following all the things that start with the /b/ sound.

TIP

As they move through the maze, have the child say the name of each picture and its beginning sound. Saying the picture name and its beginning sound helps readers identify individual sounds in words.

Letter formation b

Trace the upper case B.

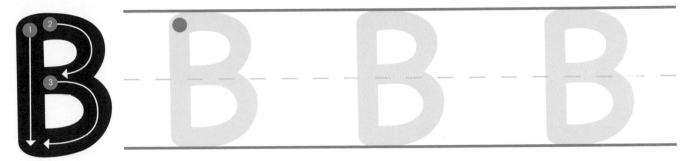

Copy the upper case B.

B

Trace the lower case b.

Copy the lower case b.

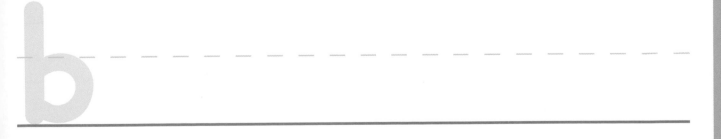

The /c/ sound

Cc

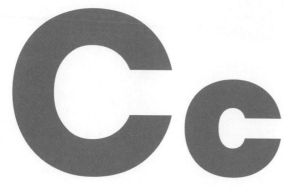

Say the
letter sound.

Circle all the things that start with the /c/ sound.

Trace the upper case C.

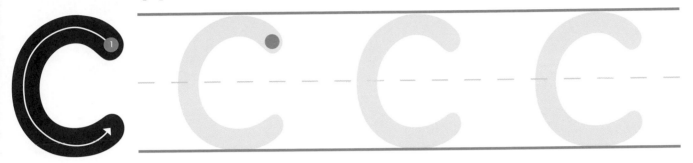

Copy the upper case C.

Trace the lower case c.

Copy the lower case c.

The /g/ sound

Gg

Say the letter sound.

Check ✓ **all the things that start with the /g/ sound.**

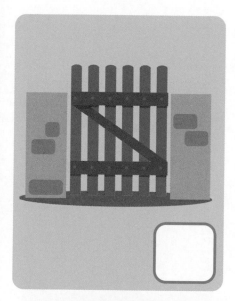

Trace the upper case G.

Copy the upper case G.

G

Trace the lower case g.

Copy the lower case g.

g

Hh

Say the letter sound.

Color all the things that start with the /h/ sound.

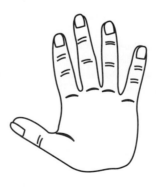

Trace the upper case H.

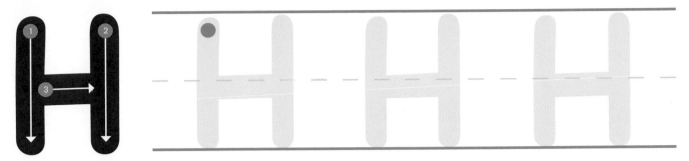

Copy the upper case H.

Trace the lower case h.

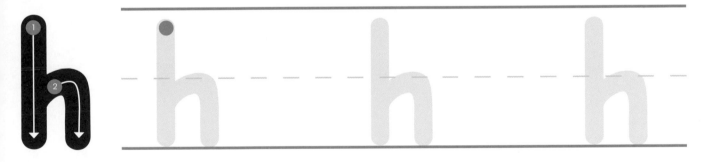

Copy the lower case h.

Here are 10 things that start with a /b/, /c/, /g/, or /h/ sound. Which of these things can you find in the big picture?

Check ✓ the things you find.

Color each shape with a thing that starts with a /b/, /c/, /g/, or /h/ sound.

TIP

For extra practice, have the child name five words that start with the /b/ sound. Do the same for words that start with /c/, /g/, and /h/. This game expands the child's vocabulary skills.

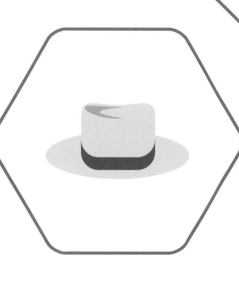

Match the upper case letter to the lower case letter.

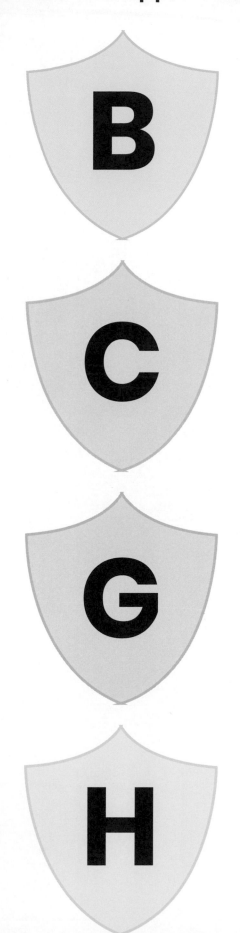

B

C

G

H

c

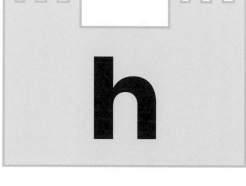

h

b

g

Match the lower case letter to the upper case letter.

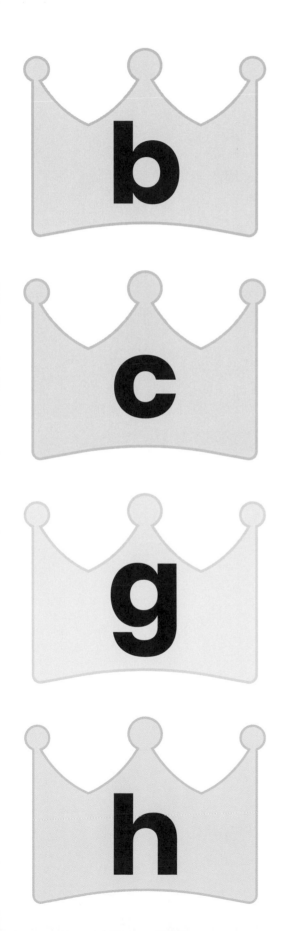

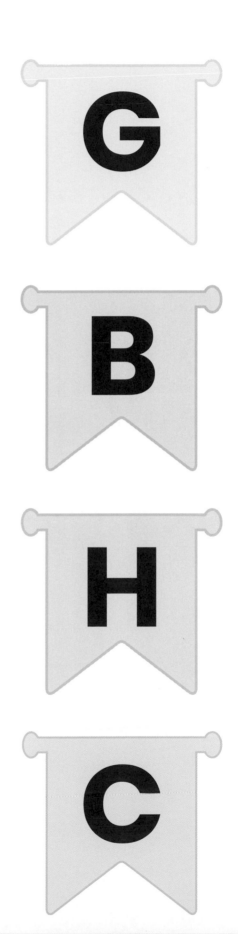

Fill in the missing sound.

___ a p

___ o p

___ a t

Fill in the missing sound.

___ a g

___ o t

___ a t

Fill in the missing sound.

c __ t

h __ p

h __ t

Fill in the missing sound.

 b _ g

 c _ p

 b _ t

Final missing sound

Fill in the missing sound.

h o __

c a __

b a __

Fill in the missing sound.

c a __

h o __

b a __

Fill in all the missing sounds.

___ ___ ___

___ ___ ___

___ ___ ___

Fill in all the missing sounds.

_ _ _ _ _ _

_ _ _ _ _ _

_ _ _ _ _ _

Trace the words to help the king, queen, and knight.

Trace the word. Then read the word.

was   was   was

Copy the word.

Trace the word. Then read the word.

when   when

Copy the word.

Trace the word. Then read the word.

word   word

Copy the word.

Trace the word. Then read the word.

hot   hot

Copy the word.

Trace the word. Then read the word.

cap   cap

Copy the word.

Trace the word. Then read the word.

hop   hop

Copy the word.

TIP

As the child is tracing the words, have them say the sound as they form each letter. Saying the sound while writing the letter strengthens reading and spelling skills.

Trace the words to make sentences. Then read the sentences.

Bob has
a cap.

When can
Bob hit?

It was hot
in the sun.

Dragon game

For 1 to 4 players. You will need tokens and a die. Take turns throwing the die and moving your token. Read the word you land on. If you land on a dragon tail, move up the dragon to its head. If you land on a dragon head, move down the dragon to its tail.

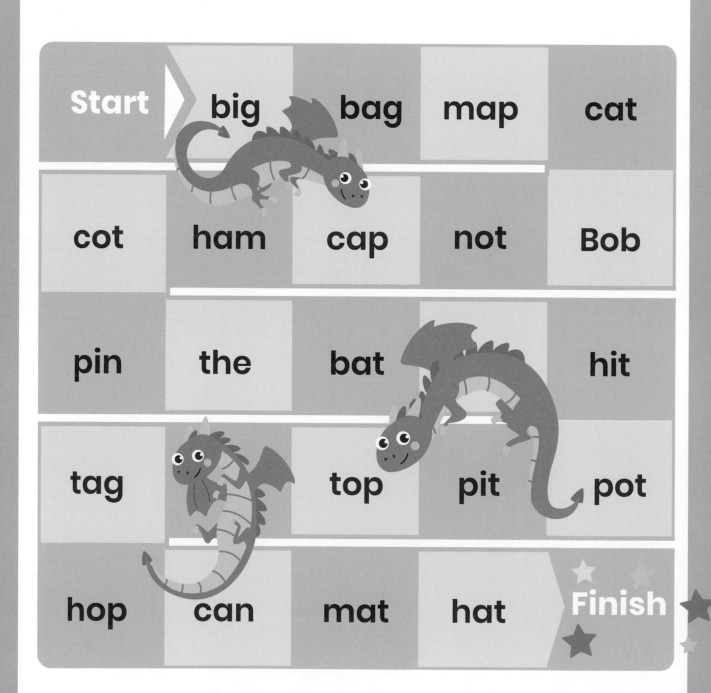

Start big bag map cat

cot ham cap not Bob

pin the bat hit

tag top pit pot

hop can mat hat **Finish**

Congratulations!

Now you know your
b c g h sounds.

Well done!

Collect a planet
sticker to add to
your journey map.

STAGE 3
COMPLETE

Have you collected all of
your letter sound stars
from the sticker page?

Bb
Cc
Gg
Hh

Dd

Say the letter sound.

Check ✓ all the things that start with the /d/ sound.

Trace the upper case D.

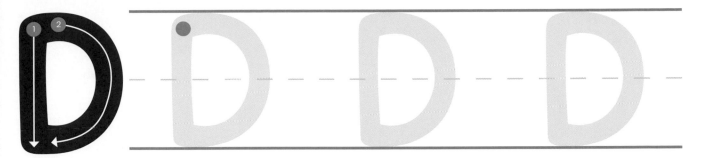

Copy the upper case D.

Trace the lower case d.

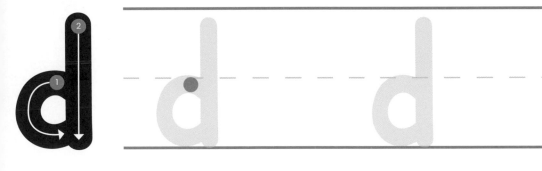

Copy the lower case d.

Ee

Say the letter sound.

Color all the things that start with the /e/ sound.

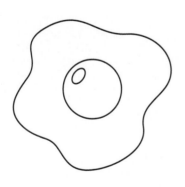

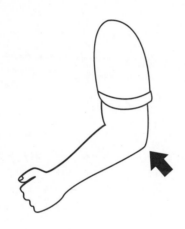

Trace the upper case E.

Copy the upper case E.

Trace the lower case e.

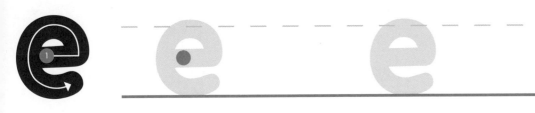

Copy the lower case e.

The /f/ sound

F f

Say the letter sound.

Circle all the things that start with the /f/ sound.

TIP

Have the child say the names of the pictures. For every word ask, "What is the first sound you hear?" Have them say the beginning sound before they start to circle the pictures.

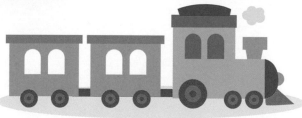

Letter formation **f**

Trace the upper case F.

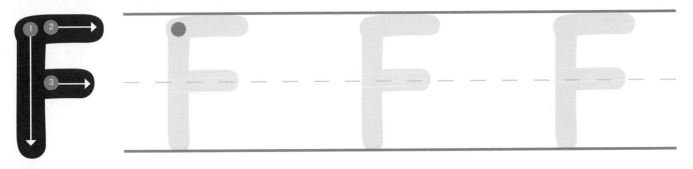

Copy the upper case F.

F

Trace the lower case f.

Copy the lower case f.

f

Vv

Say the letter sound.

Circle all the things that start with the /v/ sound.

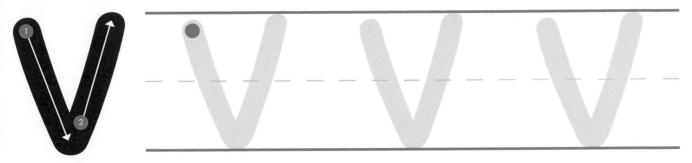

Letter formation v

Trace the upper case V.

Copy the upper case V.

Trace the lower case v.

Copy the lower case v.

Here are 10 things that start with a /d/, /e/, /f/, or /v/ sound. Which of these things can you find in the big picture?

Check  the things you find.

Color each shape with a thing that starts with a /d/, /e/, /f/, or /v/ sound.

TIP

When having the child sort sounds, have them say the picture name and the beginning sounds for each word. Saying the words and sounds out loud helps them sort accurately.

Match the upper case letter to the lower case letter.

Match the lower case letter to the upper case letter.

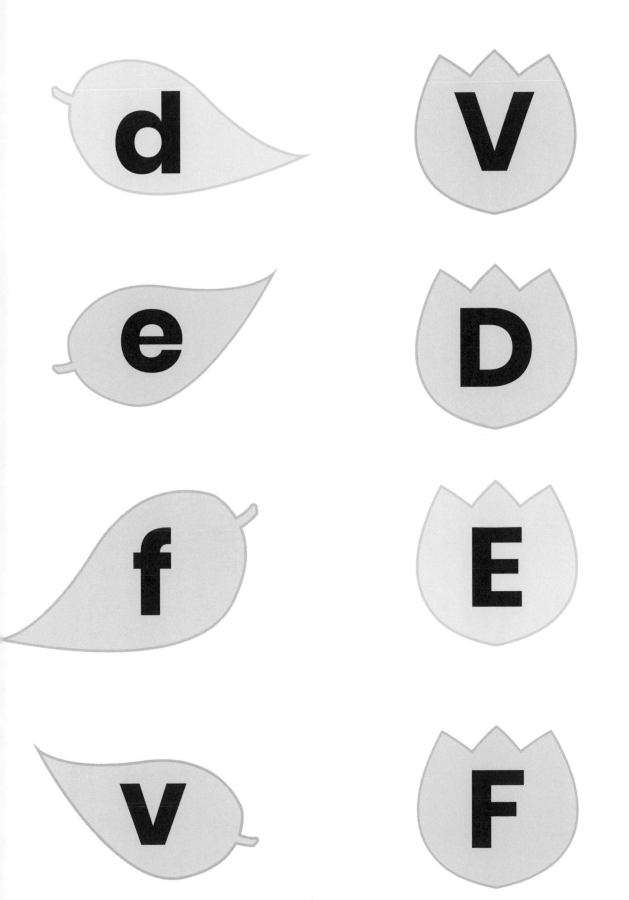

Fill in the missing sound.

 __ a n

 __ o t

 __ a n

Fill in the missing sound.

 __ i n

 __ e n

 __ e t

Fill in the missing sound.

f _ n

d _ t

v _ n

Fill in the missing sound.

f _ n

d _ n

v _ t

Fill in the missing sound.

f a __

d o __

v a __

Fill in the missing sound.

TIP

Have the child say the picture name. Ask, "What sound do you hear at the end?" After the child says the sound, ask, "What makes that sound?" Have them write the letter and read the word.

f i _

d e _

v e _

Fill in all the missing sounds.

___ ___ ___

___ ___ ___

___ ___ ___

All missing sounds

Fill in all the missing sounds.

_____ _____ _____

_____ _____ _____

_____ _____ _____

Trace the words to help the seeds grow into flowers.

Trace the word. Then read the word.

why why why

Copy the word.

Trace the word. Then read the word.

to to to

Copy the word.

Trace the word. Then read the word.

where where

Copy the word.

Trace the word. Then read the word.

dog   dog

Copy the word.

Trace the word. Then read the word.

dot   dot

Copy the word.

Trace the word. Then read the word.

fan   fan

Copy the word.

Trace the word. Then read the word.

vet   vet

Copy the word.

Trace the words to make sentences. Then read the sentences.

It is Dan.

Dan has a dog.

Dan and the dog go to the vet.

Word search

Read the words, then find them in the word search.

Check each word once you find it.

TIP
If the child cannot read each word automatically, have them sound out each letter and put the sounds together to read the word.

☐ **dig**   ☐ **cat**   ☐ **vat**

☐ **fed**   ☐ **pen**   ☐ **dog**

d	i	g	x	r
p	c	t	s	b
e	f	e	d	c
n	r	d	o	a
d	o	g	t	t
b	n	t	i	n
s	v	a	t	c

Congratulations!

Now you know your **d e f v** sounds.

Well done!

Collect a planet sticker to add to your journey map.

STAGE 4 COMPLETE

Have you collected all of your letter sound stars from the sticker page?

Dd Ee Ff Vv

The /k/ sound

Kk

Say the letter sound.

Check all the things that start with the /k/ sound.

Trace the upper case K.

Copy the upper case K.

Trace the lower case k.

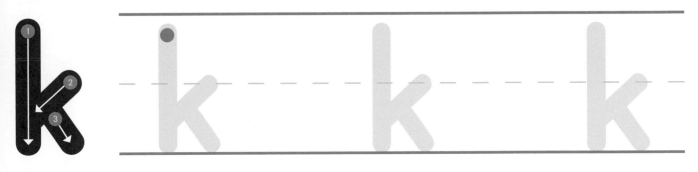

Copy the lower case k.

Ll

Say the letter sound.

Color all the things that start with the /l/ sound.

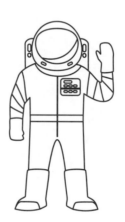

TIP

Model the /l/ sound by having the child look at your mouth as you make the sound. Say, "See how my tongue is behind my teeth and I am using my voice."

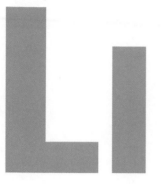

Trace the upper case L.

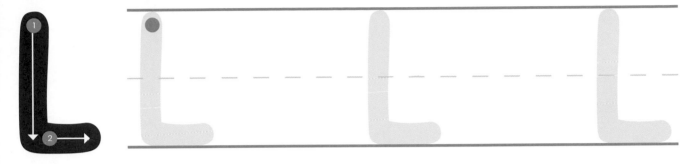

Copy the upper case L.

Trace the lower case l.

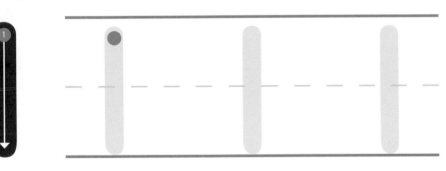

Copy the lower case l.

Rr

Say the letter sound.

Circle all the things that start with the /r/ sound.

Trace the upper case R.

Copy the upper case R.

Trace the lower case r.

Copy the lower case r.

Say the letter sound.

Circle all the things that start with the /u/ sound.

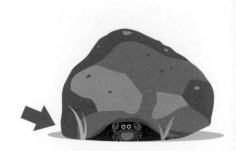

Trace the upper case U.

Copy the upper case U.

Trace the lower case u.

Copy the lower case u.

Circle the four things that begin with a /k/, /l/, /r/, or /u/ sound that do not belong in the picture.

TIP

Before this activity, discuss things found on the ocean floor. Have the child name some things they would and wouldn't find. This engages their background knowledge and prepares them for sorting.

Color each shell with a thing that starts with a /k/, /l/, /r/, or /u/ sound.

Match the upper case letter to the lower case letter.

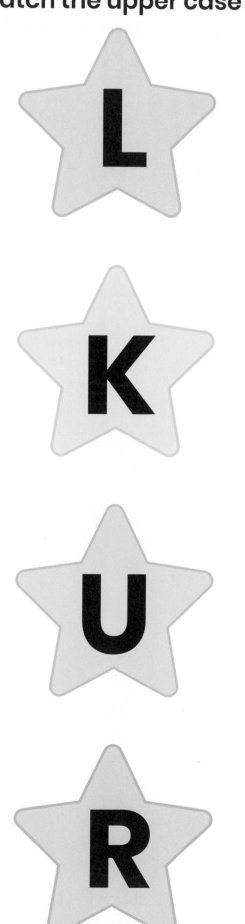

Match the lower case letter to the upper case letter.

u

L

i

R

r

K

k

U

Fill in the missing sound.

_ u g

_ e g

_ u n

Fill in the missing sound.

__ i d

__ a t

__ i d

Fill in the missing sound.

r __ t

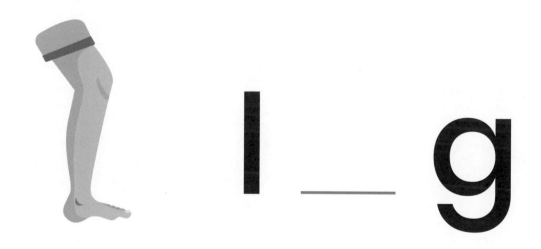

l __ g

r __ g

Fill in the missing sound.

l _ d

s _ n

k _ d

Fill in the missing sound.

 r a __

 s u __

 l e __

Fill in the missing sound.

 l i __

 r u __

 k i __

STAGE 5 : k l r u

Fill in all the missing sounds.

___ ___ ___

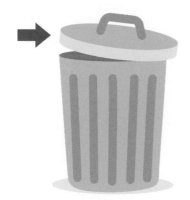

___ ___ ___

___ ___ ___

Fill in all the missing sounds.

_____ _____ _____

_____ _____ _____

_____ _____ _____

Trace the words to help the diver find the sea creatures.

TIP

Point out the regular and irregular parts of the heart words before the child writes them. Have them say the sound as they write the letter(s).

Trace the word. Then read the word.

no　　no　　no

Copy the word.

Trace the word. Then read the word.

I　I　I

Copy the word.

Trace the word. Then read the word.

what　what

Copy the word.

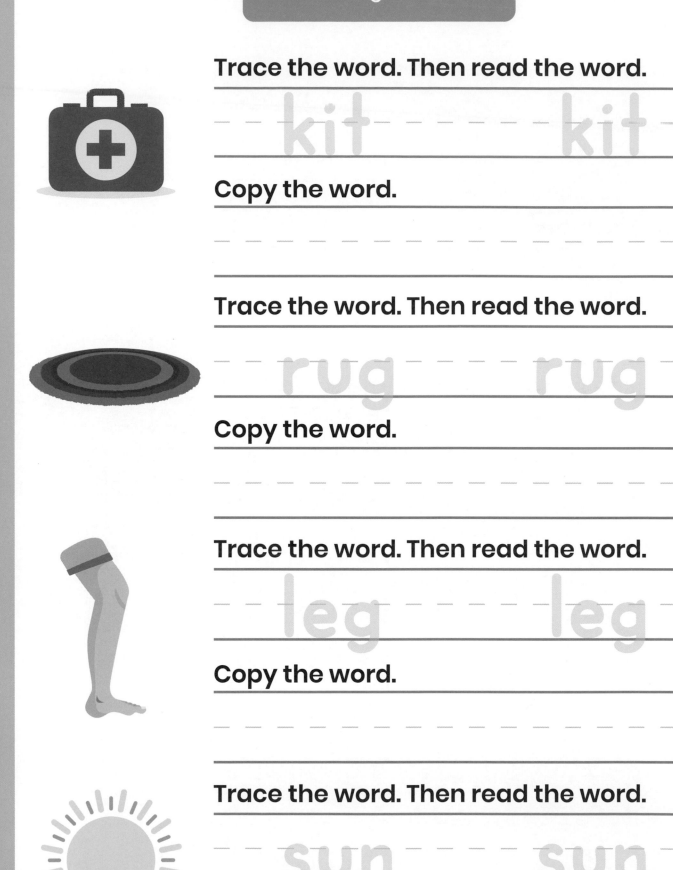

Trace the word. Then read the word.

kit   kit

Copy the word.

Trace the word. Then read the word.

rug   rug

Copy the word.

Trace the word. Then read the word.

leg   leg

Copy the word.

Trace the word. Then read the word.

sun   sun

Copy the word.

Trace the words to make sentences. Then read the sentences.

I am Lin.

Lin has a kit.

Lin can run!

Fishing game

Color the fish with the /k/ sound red. Color the fish with the /l/ sound green. Color the fish with the /r/ sound yellow. Color the fish with the /u/ sound blue.

TIP

Have the child read the words out loud and name the sounds before starting to color. Be sure that they say each sound correctly. For example, /k/ not /kuh/ and /r/ not /er/.

Congratulations!

Now you know your **k l r u** sounds.

Well done!

Collect a planet sticker to add to your journey map.

STAGE 5 COMPLETE

Have you collected all of your letter sound stars from the sticker page?

Kk Ll Rr Uu

Jj

Say the letter sound.

Get the player to the goal by following all the things that start with the /j/ sound.

Trace the upper case J.

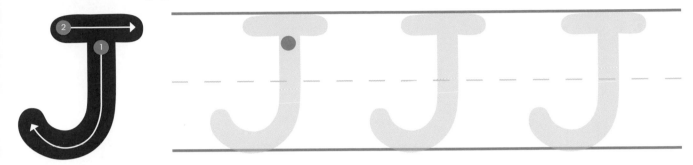

Copy the upper case J.

Trace the lower case j.

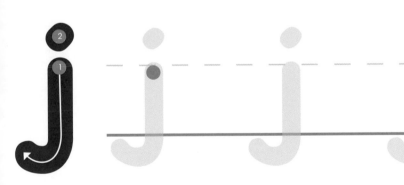

Copy the lower case j.

The /w/ sound

Ww

Say the letter sound.

Circle the thing in each row that starts with the /w/ sound.

136

Trace the upper case W.

Copy the upper case W.

Trace the lower case w.

Copy the lower case w.

Zz

Say the letter sound.

Circle all the things that start with the /z/ sound.

TIP

The /z/ and /s/ sounds are made the same way in your mouth. However, the /z/ sound uses your voice and the /s/ sound only uses air. Have the child say each sound to find the differences.

Trace the upper case Z.

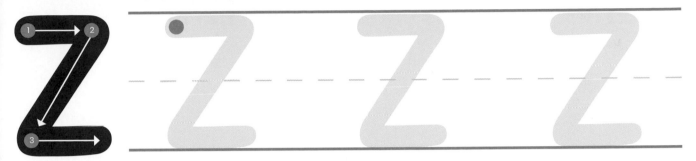

Copy the upper case Z.

Trace the lower case z.

Copy the lower case z.

Sorting sounds

Here are 10 things that start with a /j/, /w/, or /z/ sound. Which of these things can you find in the big picture?

Check the things you find.

Color each section that has a thing that starts with a /j/, /w/, or /z/ sound.

Match the upper case letter to the lower case letter.

TIP

When matching letters, ensure that the child is saying the letter sounds first to build the letter-sound relationship. Ensure that they only say the consonant sound (example: the /j/ sound is /j/ not /juh/).

Matching lower and upper case

Match the lower case letter to the upper case letter.

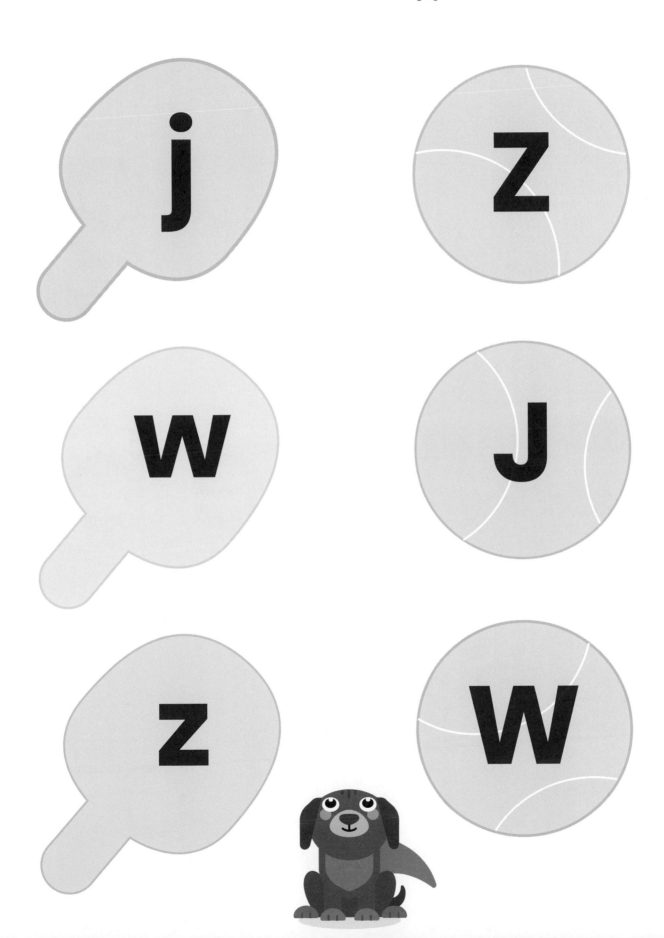

Fill in the missing sound.

___ u g

___ e b

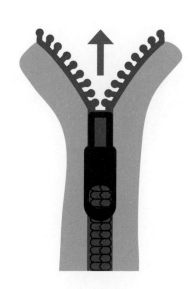

___ i p

Fill in the missing sound.

___ e t

___ o g

___ i n

Fill in the missing sound.

w __ b

w __ n

z __ p

Fill in the missing sound.

j _ g

w _ t

j _ g

Final missing sound

Fill in the missing sound.

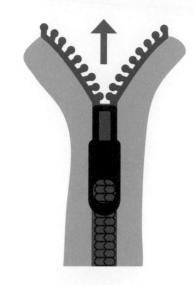

zi __

we __

ju __

Fill in the missing sound.

 we__

 jo__

 wi__

Fill in all the missing sounds.

_____   _____   _____

_____   _____   _____

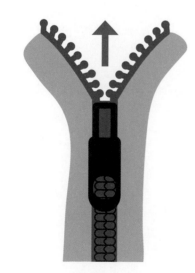

_____   _____   _____

Fill in all the missing sounds.

_____ __ ____

_____ __ ____

_____ __ ____

Trace the words to help the player get to the ball.

so

which

once

Heart words

Trace the word. Then read the word.

so   so   so

Copy the word.

Trace the word. Then read the word.

which   which

Copy the word.

Trace the word. Then read the word.

once   once

Copy the word.

Trace the word. Then read the word.

wet   wet

Copy the word.

Trace the word. Then read the word.

jog   jog

Copy the word.

Trace the word. Then read the word.

log   log

Copy the word.

Trace the words to make sentences. Then read the sentences.

It is Jim.

Jim was on a log.

Jim can jog, but it is so wet.

Board game

For 1 to 4 players. You will need tokens and a die. Take turns throwing the die and moving your token.
Read the word you land on. If you land on a popped ball, you miss a turn.
The winner is the first person to the goal.

TIP

Before playing the game, have the child read the words on the game board. This is good practice so they can read the words more fluently as they play the game.

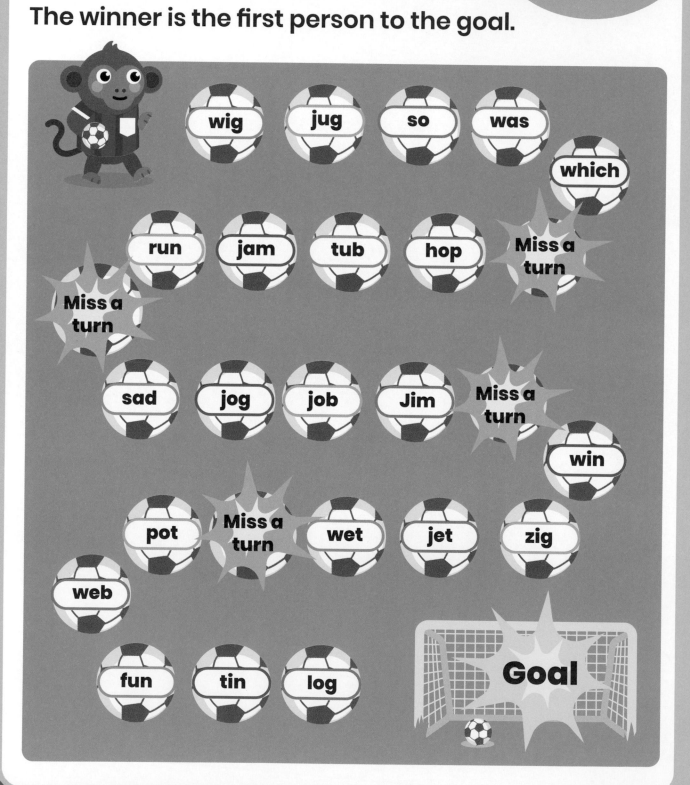

wig • jug • so • was • which

Miss a turn • run • jam • tub • hop • Miss a turn

sad • jog • job • Jim • Miss a turn • win

web • pot • Miss a turn • wet • jet • zig

fun • tin • log • **Goal**

Congratulations!

Now you know your **j w z** sounds.

Well done!

Collect a planet sticker to add to your journey map.

STAGE 6
COMPLETE

Have you collected all of your letter sound stars from the sticker page?

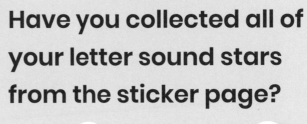

Jj

Zz

Ww

The /x/ sound

Xx

Say the letter sound.

Check ✓ all the things that end with the /x/ sound.

Trace the upper case X.

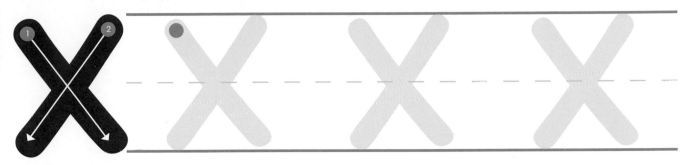

Copy the upper case X.

Trace the lower case x.

Copy the lower case x.

Yy

Say the letter sound.

Color all the things that start with the /y/ sound.

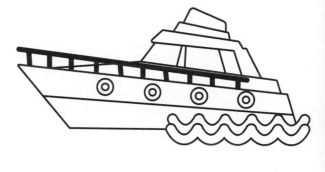

TIP

The /y/ sound is tricky to say alone. Practice saying words that begin with the /y/ sound. Then have the child say the /y/ sound individually.

Trace the upper case Y.

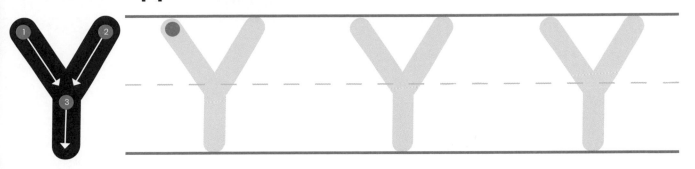

Copy the upper case Y.

Trace the lower case y.

Copy the lower case y.

Sorting sounds

Here are 10 things that start with a /y/ sound, or end with an /x/, /ll/, /ff/, /ss/, or /zz/ sound. Which of these things can you find in the big picture?

Check ✓ the things you find.

Circle the animal with the /x/ sound to reveal which animal is hiding in the box.

Match the upper case letter to the lower case letter.

Match the lower case letter to the upper case letter.

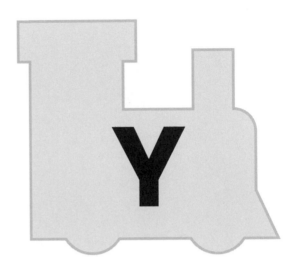

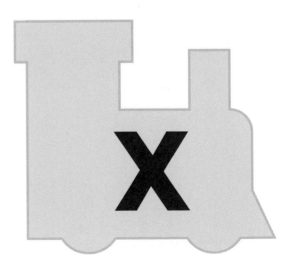

Fill in the missing sound.

___ o ll

___ o x

___ u zz

Fill in the missing sound.

6 __ i x

 __ a k

 __ i ss

Fill in the missing sound.

k __ ss

f __ x

y __ k

Fill in the missing sound.

b __ zz

d __ ll

6 s __ x

Fill in the missing sound.

f o __

b u __

k i __

Fill in the missing sound.

 do___

6 si___

 ya___

Fill in all the missing sounds.

_____ _____ _____

_____ _____ _____

_____ _____ _____

Fill in all the missing sounds.

6 ___ ___ ___

___ ___ ___

___ ___ ___

Trace the words to put the furniture into the rooms.

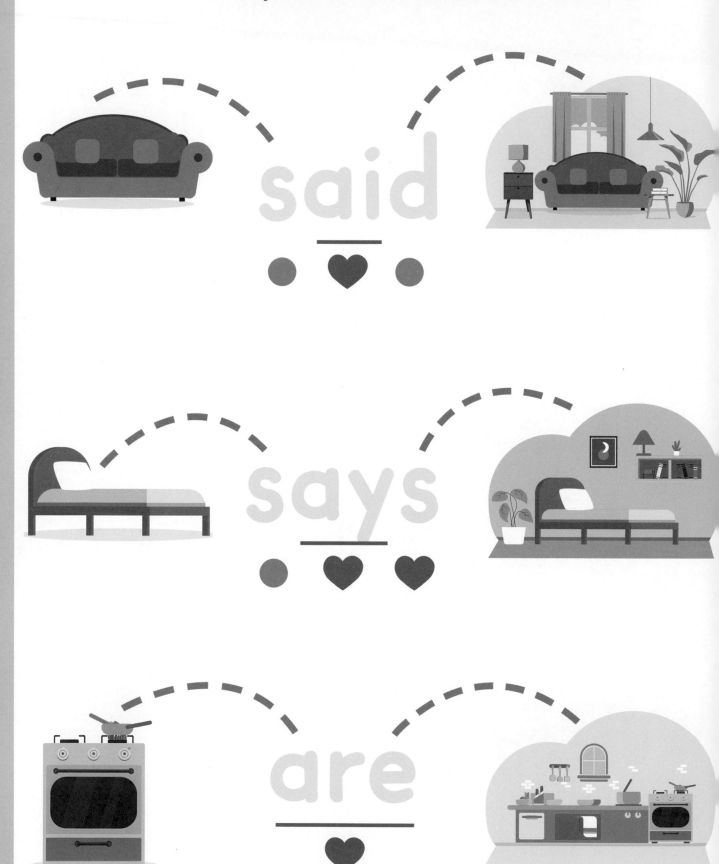

said

says

are

Trace the word. Then read the word.

said said said

Copy the word.

Trace the word. Then read the word.

says says says

Copy the word.

Trace the word. Then read the word.

are are are

Copy the word.

Trace the word. Then read the word.

yell   yell

Copy the word.

Trace the word. Then read the word.

pal   pal

Copy the word.

Trace the word. Then read the word.

off   off

Copy the word.

Trace the words to make sentences. Then read the sentences.

Rex yells to his pal.

Lin says he is a pal.

Rex was not sad.

177

Find the stickers of the things that start with a /y/ or end with an /x/ sound on the sticker page. Match the sticker with the correct word on the picture below.

yak

fox

ox

TIP

Before starting the sticker game, practice saying words that start with the /y/ sound ("yummy," "yak," "yesterday"). Then, practice saying words that end with the /k/ /s/ sounds ("box," "fix," "Max").

Congratulations!

Now you know your
x y ff ll ss zz sounds.

Well done!

Collect a planet
sticker to add to
your journey map.

STAGE 7 COMPLETE

Have you collected all of
your letter sound stars
from the sticker page?

Xx   Yy   ff   ll   ss   zz

STAGE 1 : s a t i m

Page 8

Page 10

Page 12

Page 14

Page 16

Page 18

Page 19

Page 20

Page 21

Page 22

 m a t

 s i t

 s a t

Page 23

 s i <u>i</u> t

 s <u>a</u> t

 m <u>a</u> t

Page 24

 s a <u>t</u>

 m a <u>t</u>

 s i <u>t</u>

Page 25

 m a <u>t</u>

 s i <u>t</u>

 s <u>a</u> t

Page 32

Page 34

Page 36

Page 38

Page 39

Page 40

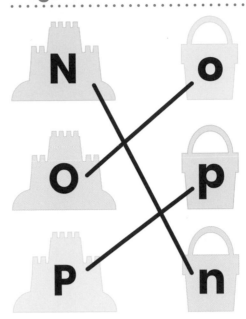

Page 41

Page 42

 map

 pot

 pop

Page 43

 top

 nap

 pan

Page 44

 pop

 nap

 map

Page 45

 top

 pot

 pan

Page 46

 top

 map

 pop

Page 47

 pot

pan

 nap

Page 48

 map

 pot

 pop

Page 49

 top

 nap

 pan

Page 54

Page 56

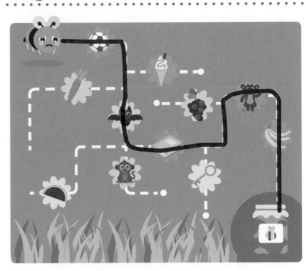

Page 58

Page 60

Page 62

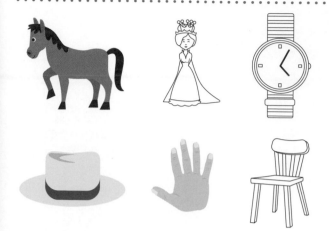

Page 64

Page 65

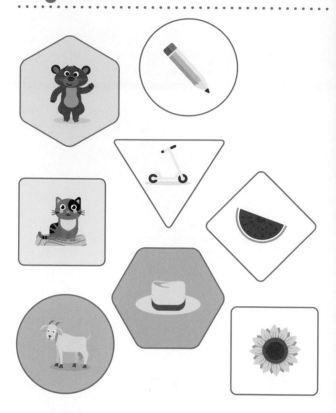

Page 66

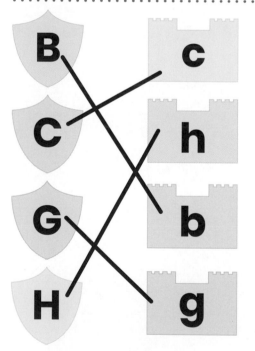

Page 67

b ⟍ G
c ✕ B
g ✕ H
h ⟋ C

Page 68

c a p

h o p

b a t

Page 69

b a g

h o t

c a t

Page 70

c a t

h o p

h o t

Page 71

b a g

c a p

b a t

Page 72

h o t

c a p

b a g

Page 73

 c a t

 h o p

 b a t

Page 74

 c a p

 h o p

 b a t

Page 75

 b a g

 h o t

 c a t

Page 82

Page 84

Page 86

Page 88

Page 90

Page 91

Page 92

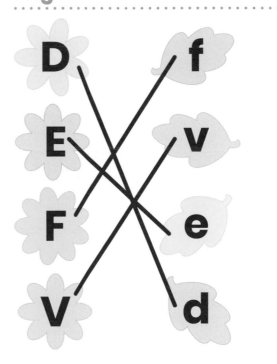

Page 93

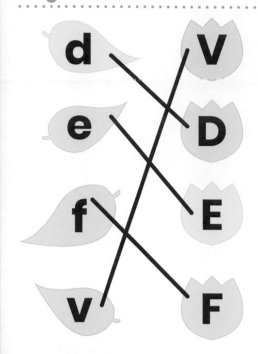

Page 94

 f a n

 d o t

 v a n

Page 95

 f i n

 d e n

 v e t

Page 96

 f a n

 d o t

 v a n

Page 97

 f i n

 d e n

 v e t

Page 98

 f a n

 d o t

 v a n

Page 99

 f i n

 d e n

 v e t

Page 100

 f a n

 d o t

 v a n

Page 101

 f i n

 d e n

 v e t

Page 106

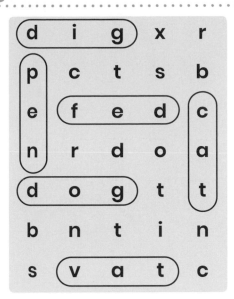

STAGE 5 : k l r u

Page 107

Page 110

191

Page 112

Page 114

Page 116

Page 117

Page 118

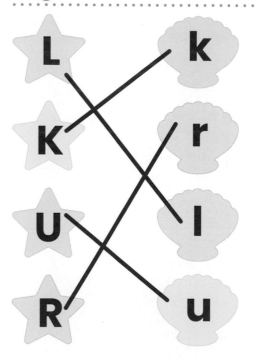

Page 119

Page 120

r u g

l e g

s u n

Page 121

k i d

r a t

lid

Page 122

r a t

l e g

r u g

Page 123

l i d

s u n

k i d

Page 124

r a t

s u n

l e g

Page 125

 l i d

 r u g

 k i d

Page 126

 l e g

 l i d

 k i d

Page 127

 r a t

 r u g

 s u n

Page 132

kin

sun

rig

kit

fig

tug

lid

bag

big

bug

kid

STAGE 6 : j w z

Page 134

Page 136

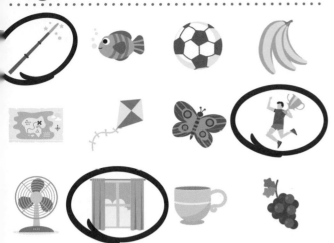

Page 138

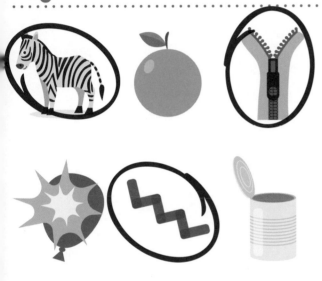

Page 140

Page 141

Page 142

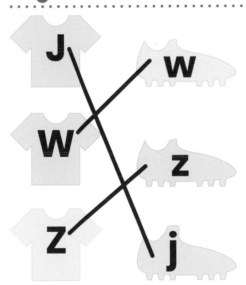

Page 143

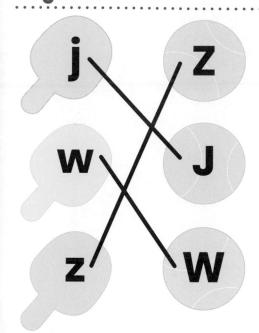

j   Z

W   J

Z   W

Page 144

 j u g

 w e b

 z i p

Page 145

 w e t

 j o g

 w i n

Page 146

 w e b

 w i n

 z i p

Page 147

 j u g

 w e t

 j o g

Page 148

 z i p

 w e t

 j u g

Page 149

 web

 jog

 **win**

Page 150

 jug

 web

 zip

Page 151

 wet

 jog

 win

Page 150

Page 160

Page 162

Page 163

Page 164

Page 165

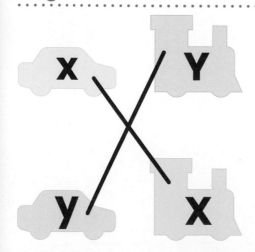

Page 166

d o ll

f o x

b u zz

Page 167

6 s i x

y a k

k i ss

Page 168

k i ss

f o x

y a k

Page 169

 b u zz

 d o ll

 6 s i x

Page 170

 f o x

 b u zz

 k i ss

Page 171

 d o ll

6 s i x

 y a k

Page 172

 d o ll

 f o x

 b u zz

Page 173

6 s i x

 y a k

 k i ss

Page 178

Congratulations!

You completed the book!

Letter Sounds STAR

Well done!

Now you know all of your letters and sounds.

Collect the letter sounds star to complete your journey map.

STICKERS FOR THE JOURNEY MAP

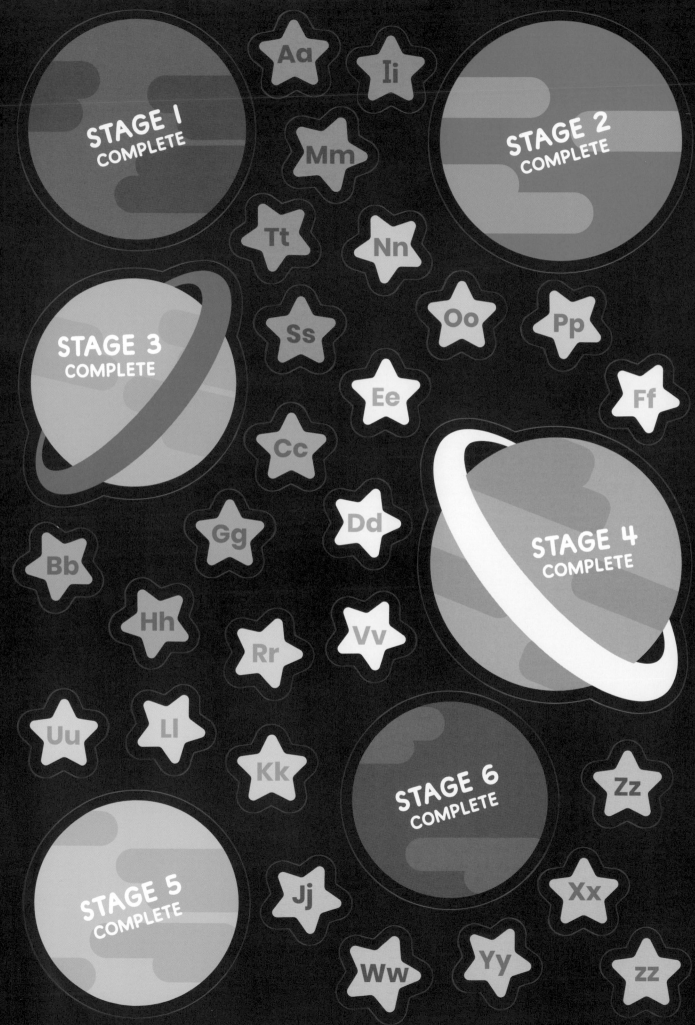

Letter Sounds STAR

ff

ss

ll

STAGE 7 COMPLETE

STICKERS FOR ACTIVITIES

Page 54

Page 178

FUN STICKERS